D0773698

Our
Christmas
Book

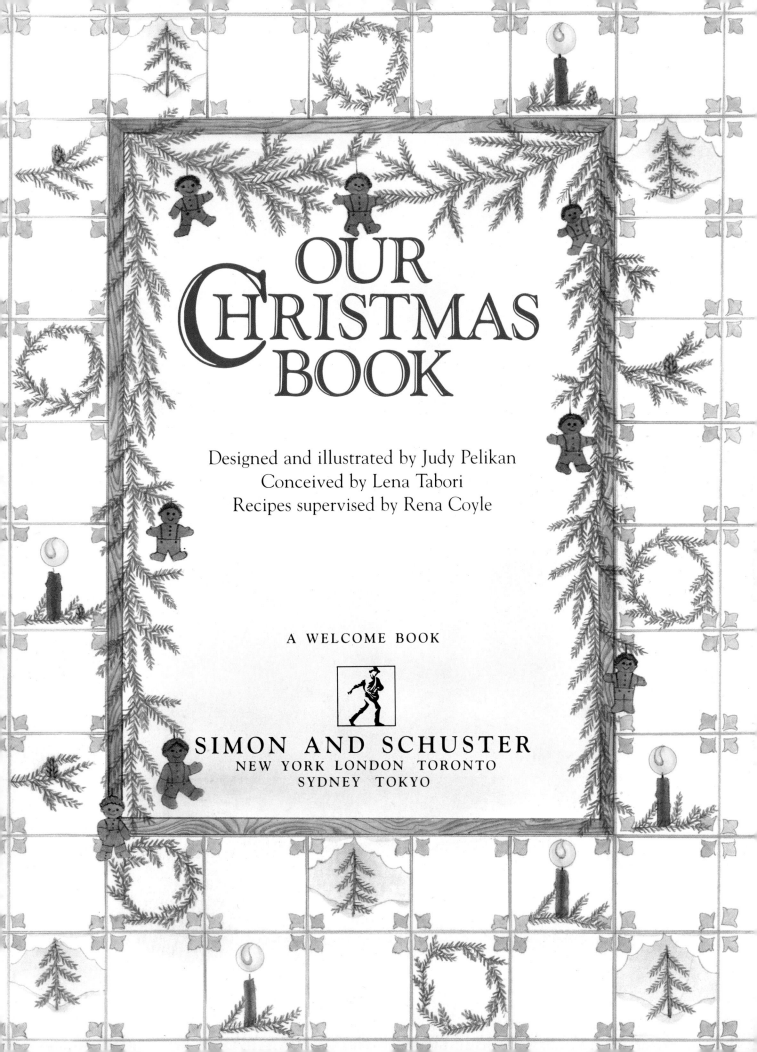

OUR CHRISTMAS BOOK

Designed and illustrated by Judy Pelikan
Conceived by Lena Tabori
Recipes supervised by Rena Coyle

A WELCOME BOOK

SIMON AND SCHUSTER
NEW YORK LONDON TORONTO
SYDNEY TOKYO

SIMON AND SCHUSTER

Edited by TIMOTHY GRAY

"The Legend of the Christmas Rose"
by Selma Lagerlöf from
The Girl from Marsh Croft
by Selma Lagerlöf, reprinted by
permission of Doubleday and Company, Inc.

Special thanks to REBECCA WOLCOTT ATWATER.

Published by Simon and Schuster
A Division of Simon & Schuster, Inc.
Simon & Schuster Building,
Rockefeller Center
1230 Avenue of the Americas,
New York, New York 10020

SIMON AND SCHUSTER and colophon are registered
trademarks of Simon & Schuster, Inc.

Produced by Welcome Enterprises, Inc., New York

Printed and bound in Singapore by Tien Wah Press

10 9 8 7 6 5 4 3 2 1

Library of Congress Catalog Card Number: 87-4474

ISBN: 0-671-64063-1

This record of our Christmas time
together will help us to treasure our holiday
memories for all the years to come.

The _____ Family

Christmas 19_____

Contents

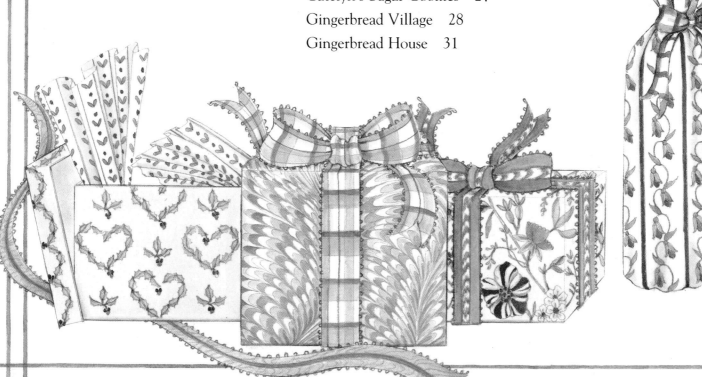

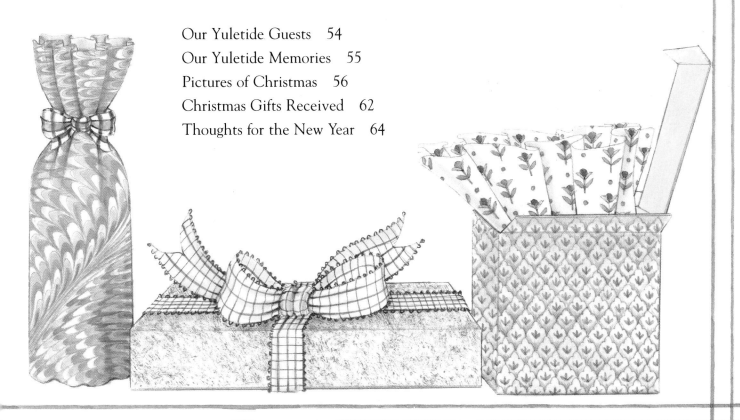

Christmas Traditions

_____
_____
_____
_____
_____
_____
_____
_____
_____
_____
_____
_____

December

Sunday	Monday	Tuesday	Wednesday

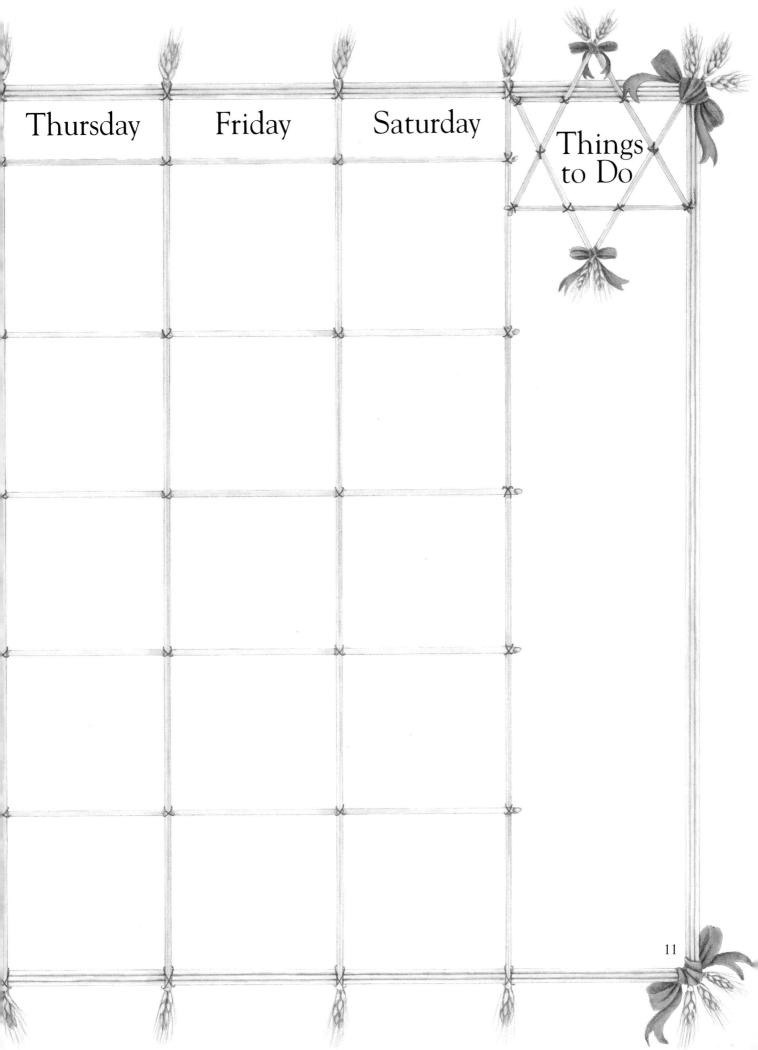

Thursday   Friday   Saturday

Things
to Do

11

A Visit from St. Nicholas

CLEMENT CLARKE MOORE

'Twas the night before Christmas, when all through the house
Not a creature was stirring, not even a mouse.
The stockings were hung by the chimney with care,
In hopes that St. Nicholas soon would be there.
The children were nestled all snug in their beds,
While visions of sugar-plums danced in their heads;
And mamma in her kerchief, and I in my cap,
Had just settled our brains for a long winter's nap—
When out on the lawn there arose such a clatter
I sprang from my bed to see what was the matter.
Away to the window I flew like a flash,
Tore open the shutter, and threw up the sash.
The moon on the breast of the new-fallen snow
Gave a lustre of midday to objects below;
When what to my wondering eye should appear
But a miniature sleigh and eight tiny reindeer,
With a little old driver, so lively and quick,
I knew in a moment it must be St. Nick!
More rapid than eagles his coursers they came,
And he whistled and shouted and called them by name.
"Now, Dasher! now, Dancer! now, Prancer and Vixen!
On, Comet! on, Cupid! on, Donder and Blitzen!—
To the top of the porch, to the top of the wall,
Now, dash away, dash away, dash away all!"

As dry leaves that before the wild hurricane fly,
When they meet with an obstacle mount to the sky,
So, up to the housetop the coursers they flew,
With a sleigh full of toys—and St. Nicholas, too.
And then, in a twinkling, I heard on the roof
The prancing and pawing of each little hoof.
As I drew in my head and was turning around,
Down the chimney St. Nicholas came with a bound:
He was dressed all in fur from his head to his foot,
And his clothes were all tarnished with ashes and soot:
A bundle of toys he had flung on his back,
And he looked like a peddler just opening his pack.
His eyes, how they twinkled! his dimples, how merry!
His cheeks were like roses, his nose like a cherry;
His droll little mouth was drawn up like a bow,
And the beard on his chin was as white as the snow.
The stump of a pipe he held tight in his teeth,
And the smoke, it encircled his head like a wreath.
He had a broad face and a little round belly
That shook, when he laughed, like a bowl full of jelly.
He was chubby and plump—a right jolly old elf:
And I laughed when I saw him, in spite of myself;
A wink of his eye, and a twist of his head,
Soon gave me to know I had nothing to dread.
He spoke not a word, but went straight to work,
And filled all the stockings: then turned with a jerk,
And laying his finger aside of his nose,
And giving a nod, up the chimney he rose.
He sprang to his sleigh, to his team gave a whistle,
And away they all flew like the down of a thistle.
But I heard him exclaim, ere they drove out of sight,
"Happy Christmas to all, and to all a good-night!"

13

Our Christmas Card List

Name and Address	Card Sent	Card Received

Name and Address

	Card Sent	Card Received

Name and Address	Card Sent	Card Received

My Secret
Christmas
Gift List

Name   Gift

Name   Gift

Christmas Drinks

Lena's Swedish Glögg

SERVES 8

1 quart port wine
¼ pound raisins
¼ pound whole blanched
   almonds
8 cardamom pods
5 whole cloves
3 cinnamon sticks

zest of one lemon, cut into strips
zest of one naval orange, cut
   into strips
½ pound mixed dried apricots,
   apples, and prunes
1 quart dry red wine
aquavit

To prepare: Pour port wine into nonaluminum saucepan with raisins and almonds. Put spices, zests, and dried fruits in strainer over pan so they are well covered by wine. (You may alter quantities to suit your taste.) Simmer over low heat for one hour. Turn off heat, cover, and let steep for one day.

    To serve: Remove strainer. (You may wish to save fruits for delicious compote.) Add dry red wine to pan. Heat mixture over low flame until very hot. Pour into glasses. Include some raisins and almonds from pan. Add a tablespoon of aquavit.

Traditional Egg Nog

SERVES 16

Ingredients
12 eggs, separated
1 cup sugar
1½ quarts heavy cream

1 quart milk
2 cups whiskey
2 cups rum
nutmeg

Beat egg yolks with sugar until light. Add cream, milk, whiskey, and rum. Blend well. Stiffly beat egg whites. Stir in. Chill for several hours. Serve with a sprinkle of nutmeg. You may wish to use either all whiskey or all rum. You can also substitute these with bourbon, brandy, dry sherry, or port.

Our Favorite
Christmas Drinks

_____
_____
_____
_____
_____
_____
_____
_____
_____
_____
_____
_____
_____
_____
_____
_____
_____
_____

A favorite Christmas toast _____
_____
_____
_____

Christmas Sweets

Cinnamon Bun Christmas Tree

MAKES 1 TREE

Christmas Day breakfast will be especially fun with this Cinnamon Bun treat. If baking in advance, let tree cool before wrapping in plastic and storing in freezer. On Christmas morning, unwrap and pop in 250° oven for 20 minutes.

INGREDIENTS

2 packages active dry yeast	½ cup white raisins	**Honey Glaze**	**White Icing**
1 cup warm milk	¾ cup pecan halves	Cream together:	Mix together:
3½ cups flour	1 grated lemon rind	¼ cup butter	¼ cup confectioner's
½ cup (1 stick) butter	2 teaspoons cinnamon	1 cup confectioner's	sugar
1¼ cups sugar	6 Tablespoons melted	sugar	1½ Tablespoons water
3 egg yolks	butter	¼ cup honey	

METHOD

1. Dissolve yeast in warm milk. Mix in ½ cup flour. Cover and put in warm place to rise (about 20 minutes).
2. Cream together butter and ¼ cup sugar. Mix in egg yolks one at a time. Gradually add remaining 3 cups flour, then raisins, pecans, and lemon rind.
3. Once yeast mixture has risen, add to dough and blend well. Knead until dough is smooth (about 7 minutes).
4. Lightly brush dough with vegetable oil. Place in bowl, cover with kitchen towel, and put in warm place. Let rise to twice the size (about 45 minutes).
5. Punch dough down and cover. Let rise another 30 to 40 minutes.
6. Punch dough down again. Cut in half. Roll each piece into rectangle 12″ by 18″. Brush each with melted butter (saving a little), then sprinkle entire surface with cinnamon and remaining 1 cup sugar. Taking longest end, roll tightly. Placing seam side down, slice buns 1½″ thick. Place four buns in a row near bottom of cookie sheet. Make sure seams face inward to prevent unraveling. Place three buns above this row so that each one nestles between tops of buns below. Do same for another row of two buns. Top off with one bun. Place a bun beneath center of bottom row for tree stump. Cover tree with kitchen towel. Set aside to rise for 30 minutes.
7. Preheat oven 350°. Brush remaining melted butter on tree.
8. Bake for 30 minutes or until dough turns golden brown. Remove and let rest 5 minutes. Spread on Honey Glaze. When nearly cool, drizzle on White Icing with tines of a fork.

Our Favorite
Christmas Sweets

_____
_____
_____
_____
_____
_____
_____
_____
_____
_____

Catelyn's Sugar Cookies

MAKES 30 COOKIES

INGREDIENTS

½ cup sugar

1 cups (2 sticks) butter

1 egg

¼ teaspoon vanilla extract

1 small orange

3 cups flour

Icing (optional)

¼ cup confectioner's sugar

1½ Tablespoons water

food coloring as needed

assorted sprinkles

METHOD

1. Cream together sugar and butter. Add eggs and vanilla. Grate orange peel using small holes of grater. Blend in. Slowly add flour. (You may wrap in plastic wrap and refrigerate until ready to use.)
2. Preheat oven 350°.
3. On lightly floured surface, roll dough to ¼″ thickness. Press cookie cutters into dough. Reroll excess dough. Place cookies on cookie sheet, set in center of oven, and bake 15 minutes or until golden brown around edges. Cool on a rack.
4. If not using icing, decorate with colored sugar crystals, chocolate fancies, silver balls, red hots, or other sprinkles before baking or immediately after removing from oven. If using icing, mix confectioner's sugar and water. Divide into separate bowls, adding food coloring to each bowl one drop at a time. Decorate with knife and/or pastry bag. Accentuate with assorted sprinkles.

Gingerbread Village

One recipe yields one complete structure in dimensions of diagram, or four small structures using half dimensions. Use excess dough for cookies or shapes of your own invention.

To create a village scene, use a piece of wood as a base to support weight. Assemble structures, varying proportions to create church, school, barn, cottage, doghouse, etc.

Roof Additions: Assemble steeple using diagram. For chimney, bell tower, or cupola, use same pattern with top cut off.

Country Roofs: For snowy roof, cover with Royal Icing. For shingled roof, cover with Royal Icing and add Necco wafers, vanilla wafers, ginger snaps, or anything else. For thatched roof, cover with Royal Icing, pull apart shreaded wheat, and sprinkle generously. For fancy roof, decorate with Royal Icing in pastry bag.

Outlines and Icicles: Place Royal Icing in pastry bag with fine tip. Outline windows, doors, or create other designs. To make icicles hang off eaves, squeeze small blob of Royal Icing onto edge, use tip of pastry bag to gently pull down until icicle tapers off.

Candy Accessories
(attach with Royal Icing)
Miniature candy canes
Peppermint drops
Gumdrops
Jelly rings
Necco wafers
Cookies
M&Ms
Life savers
Rock candy
Marzipan figures
Chocolate mint wreaths
Licorice
Jelly beans
Chocolate chips
Silver balls

Christmas Songs & Stories

Quaint fences: For posts and/or rails, use tootsie rolls, licorice sticks or shoelaces, straight ends of candy canes, leftover dough rolled and baked, or chocolate mint wafers (halved with ends pointed).

Pathways and ground: Use Royal Icing, shredded coconut, chopped nuts, rolled oats, colored sugar, or colored or chocolate sprinkles.

Snowy Hill: Crumple some paper towels, cover with foil, top with Royal Icing. Use sturdy box underneath if placing a house on top.

Stained-Glass Windows: Place assorted life savers on cutting board, crush into small bits with back of heavy pot. Place windowed wall over foil on cookie sheet. Fill window with bits. Place in preheated 350° oven 4 minutes. Remove and cool. Peel foil. For heightened effect, put small flashlight or Christmas lights inside house.

Cookie Cutouts: Attach cutouts of people, animals, and trees with Royal Icing. For 4-sided tree, slice two tree cookies lengthwise, piece together with Royal Icing.

Popcorn Trees: Cover an upside-down ice-cream cone with Royal Icing. Garnish with popcorn, gumdrops, red hots, or combinations.

Everything is edible!

PATTERNS

Make cardboard patterns for structures you are assembling.
Use measurements in illustrations or ones of equal proportions.

ROYAL ICING

Makes 3 cups

Ingredients
4 egg whites
5½ cups confectioners sugar
1 tsp. cream of Tartar

Method
1. Beat egg whites in bowl until light and fluffy.
2. Sprinkle in sugar, stir until peaks form. Sprinkle in cream of Tartar.
3. For stiffer icing, add sugar. For thinner icing, add drop of lemon juice. Add food coloring if desired. Keep bowl covered with damp cloth when not using.

ASSEMBLY

Prepare Royal Icing for "glue" to hold structures together.

Walls
Generously dab icing on side edges of two adjoining walls with a knife. Press edges together to form a corner. Do this for all four sides to create a standing base.

Roof
Generously dab icing along top of foundation. Press one roof section into position. Generously dab icing along top part of roof. Place second roof section into position. Press two sections together. If sliding occurs, prop tall glasses under eaves until icing hardens (overnight), or tie string around front and back overhangs.

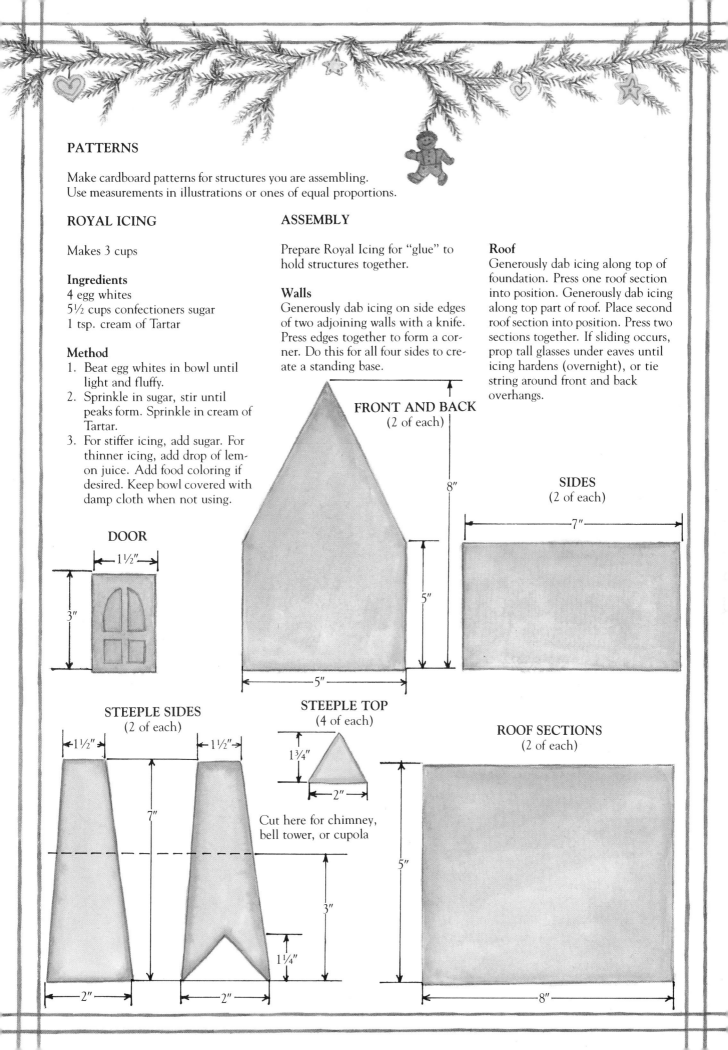

DOOR
1½″
3″

FRONT AND BACK
(2 of each)
8″
5″
5″

SIDES
(2 of each)
7″

STEEPLE SIDES
(2 of each)
1½″   1½″
7″
2″   2″

STEEPLE TOP
(4 of each)
1¾″
2″

Cut here for chimney, bell tower, or cupola
3″
1¼″

ROOF SECTIONS
(2 of each)
5″
8″

Gingerbread House

INGREDIENTS

1 cup butter (or ½ cup bacon fat
   and ½ cup butter)
2 cups sugar
1 cup molasses
1 cup heavy cream
1 T. each ground cinnamon,
   ground cloves, ground ginger
1 T. baking soda
6–7 cups all-purpose flour

METHOD

1. Cream butter with sugar. Add molasses
   and heavy cream. Blend in spices and
   baking soda. Add flour slowly until
   dough is stiff. Remove to a lightly floured
   surface. Knead until dough is smooth.
   Refrigerate in plastic wrap for 30 minutes.

2. Preheat oven 350°. Roll dough on lightly
   floured surface to ¼" thickness. Using
   patterns, cut shapes. Place on cookie
   sheet, bake 15 minutes or until edges
   brown. Check often, as smaller pieces
   bake faster. Remove and place on
   counter. While still warm, cut out windows and doors to your liking. For clap-
   board siding or brick effect, gently make
   impressions with a knife. Trim excess
   dough for straight edges. Let cool, then
   make stained-glass windows before
   assembling.

Joy to the World!

WORDS: ISAAC WATTS (1674–1748)

MUSIC: G.F. HANDEL

1. Joy to the world! the Lord is come; Let earth re- ceive her King; Let
2. Joy to the world! the Sav- iour reigns; Let men their songs em- ploy; While
3. He rules the world with truth and grace, And makes the na- tions prove The

ev- 'ry _ heart _ pre- pare _ Him_ room, _ And heav'n and na- ture sing, And
fields and_ floods,_ rocks, hills _and _ plains_ Re- peat the sound-ing joy, Re-
glo- ries of _ His right- eous- ness, _ And won- ders of His_ love, And

heav'n and na- ture_ sing, And heav'n, _ and heav _'n and na- ture sing.
peat the sound-ing _ joy, Re- peat _ re- peat_ the sound- ing joy.
won- ders of His_ love, And won- ders, and won - ders of His love.

Silent Night

Serenely

Si - lent night, ho - ly night, all is calm,

all is bright round yon vir - gin mo - ther and child

Ho - ly in - fant so ten - der and mild, sleep in heav - en - ly

peace. _____ sleep ____ in hea - ven - ly peace.

2. Silent night, holy night,
   Shepherds quake at the sight,
   Glories stream from heaven afar,
   Heav'nly hosts sing alleluia;
   Christ, the Savior is born!
   Christ, the Savior is born!

3. Silent night, holy night,
   Son of God, love's pure light
   Radiant beams from thy holy face,
   With the dawn of redeeming grace,
   Jesus, Lord, at thy birth,
   Jesus, Lord, at thy birth.

JOSEPH MOHR (1792–1848)   FRANZ XAVIER GRUBER (1787–1863)

Good King Wenceslas

Lively

Good King Wen-ces-las looked out, on the Feast of Ste-phen,

when the snow lay round a-bout, deep, and crisp, and e-ven:

Bright-ly shone the moon that night, though the frost was cru-el,

when a poor man came in sight, gath-'ring win-ter fu-el.

WORDS: JOHN MASON NEALE (1853) MUSIC: PIAE CANTIONES, 1582

Deck the Halls

1. Deck the halls with boughs of holly,
2. See the blaz-ing yule be-fore us,
3. Fast a-way the old year pass-es.

Fa-la-la-la-la, la-la-la-la;

'Tis the sea-son to be jol-ly,
Strike the harp and join the cho-rus,
Hail the new, ye lads and lass-es,

Fa-la-la-la-la, la-la-la-la.

Don we now our gay ap-par-el,
Fol-low me in mer-ry mea-sure,
Sing we joy-ous songs to-geth-er,

Fa-la-la, fa-la-la, la-la-la.

Troll the an-cient Christ-mas car-ol,
While I tell of Christ-mas trea-sure,
Heed-less of the wind and weath-er,

Fa-la-la-la-la, la-la-la-la!

with octaves ad lib. _ _ _ _ _ _ _ _ _ _ _ _ _

OLD WELSH

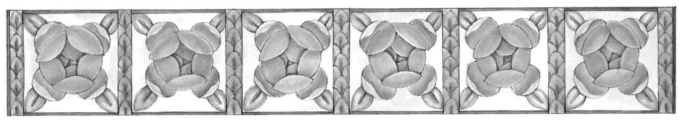

The Legend of the Christmas Rose

SELMA LAGERLÖF

Robber Mother, who lived in Robbers' Cave up in Göinge forest, went down to the village one day on a begging tour. Robber Father, who was an outlawed man, did not dare to leave the forest. She took with her five youngsters, and each youngster bore a sack on his back as long as himself. When Robber Mother stepped inside the door of a cabin, no one dared refuse to give her whatever she demanded; for she was not above coming back the following night and setting fire to the house if she had not been well received. Robber Mother and her brood were worse than a pack of wolves, and many a man felt like running a spear through them; but it was never done, because they all knew that the man stayed up in the forest, and he would have known how to wreak vengeance if anything had happened to the children or the old woman.

Now that Robber Mother went from house to house and begged, she came to Övid, which at that time was a cloister. She rang the bell of the cloister gate and asked for food. The watchman let down a small wicket in the gate and handed her six round bread cakes—one for herself and one for each of the five children.

While the mother was standing quietly at the gate, her youngsters were running about. And now one of them came and pulled at her skirt, as a signal that he had discovered something which she ought to come and see, and Robber Mother followed him promptly.

The entire cloister was surrounded by a high and strong wall, but the youngster had managed to find a little back gate which stood ajar. When Robber Mother got there, she pushed the gate open and walked inside without asking leave, as it was her custom to do.

Övid Cloister was managed at that time by Abbot Hans, who knew all about herbs. Just within the cloister wall he had planted a little herb garden, and it was into this that the old woman had forced her way.

At first glance Robber Mother was so astonished that she paused at the gate. It was high summertide, and Abbot Hans' garden was so full of flowers that the eyes were fairly dazzled by the

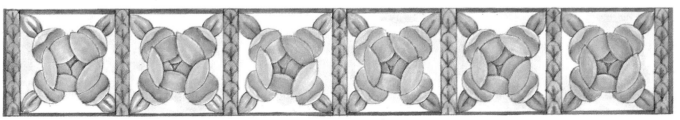

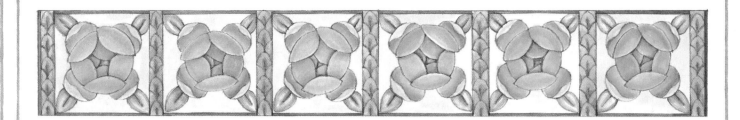

blues, reds, and yellows, as one looked into it. But presently an indulgent smile spread over her features, and she started to walk up a narrow path that lay between many flower beds.

In the garden a lay brother walked about, pulling up weeds. It was he who had left the door in the wall open, that he might throw the weeds and tares on the rubbish heap outside.

When he saw Robber Mother coming in, with all five youngsters in tow, he ran toward her at once and ordered them away. But the beggar woman walked right on as before. The lay brother knew of no other remedy than to run into the cloister and call for help.

He returned with two stalwart monks, and Robber Mother saw that now it meant business! She let out a perfect volley of shrieks, and, throwing herself upon the monks, clawed and bit at them; so did all the youngsters. The men soon learned that she could overpower them, and all they could do was go back into the cloister for reinforcements.

As they ran through the passage-way which led to the cloister, they met Abbot Hans, who came rushing out to learn what all this noise was about.

He upbraided them for using force and forbade their calling for help. He sent both monks back to their work, and although he was an old and fragile man, he took with him only the lay brother.

He came up to the woman and asked in a mild tone if the garden pleased her.

Robber Mother turned defiantly toward Abbot Hans, for she expected only to be trapped and overpowered. But when she noticed his white hair and bent form, she answered peaceably, "First, when I saw this, I thought I had never seen a prettier garden; but now I see that it can't be compared with one I know of. If you could see the garden of which I am thinking you would uproot all the flowers planted here and cast them away like weeds."

The Abbot's assistant was hardly less proud of the flowers than the Abbot himself, and after hearing her remarks he laughed derisively.

Robber Mother grew crimson with rage to think that her word was doubted, and she cried out: "You monks, who are holy men, certainly must know that on every Christmas Eve the great Göinge forest is transformed into a beautiful garden, to commemorate the hour of our Lord's birth. We who live in the forest have seen this happen every year. And in that garden I have seen flowers so lovely that I dared not lift my hand to pluck them."

Ever since his childhood, Abbot Hans had heard it said that on every Christmas Eve the forest was dressed in holiday glory. He had often longed to see it, but he had never had the good fortune. Eagerly he begged and implored Robber Mother that he might come up to the Robbers' Cave on Christmas Eve. If she would only send one of her children to show him the way, he could ride up there alone, and he would never betray them—on the contrary, he would reward them insofar as it lay in his power.

Robber Mother said no at first, for she was thinking of Robber Father and of the peril which might befall him should she permit Abbot Hans to ride up to their cave. At the same time the desire to prove to the monk that the garden which she knew was more beautiful than his got the better of her, and she gave in.

"But more than one follower you cannot take with you," said she, "and you are not to waylay us or trap us, as sure as you are a holy man."

This Abbot Hans promised, and then Robber Mother went her way.

It happened that Archbishop Absalon from

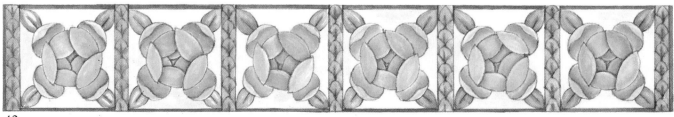

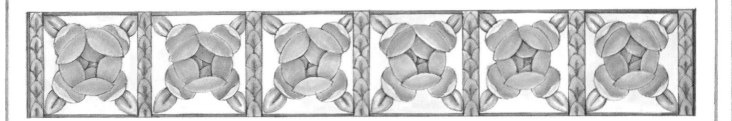

Lund came to Övid and remained through the night. The lay brother heard Abbot Hans telling the Bishop about Robber Father and asking him for a letter of ransom for the man, that he might lead an honest life among respectable folk.

But the Archbishop replied that he did not care to let the robber loose among honest folk in the villages. It would be best for all that he remain in the forest.

Then Abbot Hans grew zealous and told the Bishop all about Göinge forest, which, every year at Yuletide, clothed itself in summer bloom around the Robbers' Cave. "If these bandits are not so bad but that God's glories can be made manifest to them, surely we cannot be too wicked to experience the same blessing."

The Archbishop knew how to answer Abbot Hans. "This much I will promise you, Abbot Hans," he said, smiling, "that any day you send me a blossom from the garden in Göinge forest, I will give you letters of ransom for all the outlaws you may choose to plead for."

The following Christmas Eve Abbot Hans was on his way to the forest. One of Robber Mother's wild youngsters ran ahead of him, and close behind him was the lay brother.

It turned out to be a long and hazardous ride. They climbed steep and slippery side paths, crawled over swamp and marsh, and pushed through windfall and bramble. Just as daylight was waning, the robber boy guided them across a forest meadow, skirted by tall, naked leaf trees and green fir trees. Back of the meadow loomed a mountain wall, and in this wall they saw a door of thick boards. Now Abbot Hans understood that they had arrived, and dismounted. The child opened the heavy door for him, and he looked into a poor mountain grotto, with bare stone

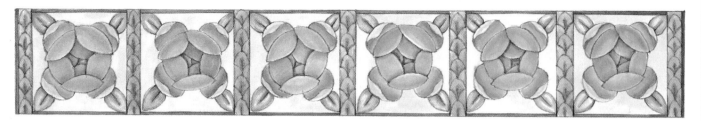

walls. Robber Mother was seated before a log fire that burned in the middle of the floor. Alongside the walls were beds of virgin pine and moss, and on one of these beds lay Robber Father asleep.

"Come in, you out there!" shouted Robber Mother without rising, "and fetch the horses in with you, so they won't be destroyed by the night cold."

Abbot Hans walked boldly into the cave, and the lay brother followed. Here were wretchedness and poverty! and nothing was done to celebrate Christmas.

Robber Mother spoke in a tone as haughty and dictatorial as any well-to-do peasant woman. "Sit down by the fire and warm yourself, Abbot Hans," said she; "and if you have food with you, eat, for the food which we in the forest prepare you wouldn't care to taste. And if you are tired after the long journey, you can lie down on one of these beds to sleep. You needn't be afraid of oversleeping, for I'm sitting here by the fire keeping watch. I shall awaken you in time to see that which you have come up here to see."

Abbot Hans obeyed Robber Mother and brought forth his food sack; but he was so fatigued after the journey he was hardly able to eat, and as soon as he could stretch himself on the bed, he fell asleep.

The lay brother was also assigned a bed to rest and he dropped into a doze.

When he woke up, he saw that Abbot Hans had left his bed and was sitting by the fire talking with Robber Mother. The outlawed robber sat also by the fire. He was a tall, raw-boned man with a dull, sluggish appearance. His back was turned to Abbot Hans, as though he would have it appear that he was not listening to the conversation.

Abbot Hans was telling Robber Mother all about the Christmas preparations he had seen on the journey, reminding her of Christmas feasts and games which she must have known in her youth, when she lived at peace with mankind.

At first Robber Mother answered in short, gruff sentences, but by degrees she became more subdued and listened more intently. Suddenly Robber Father turned toward Abbot Hans and shook his clenched fist in his face. "You miserable monk! did you come here to coax from me my wife and children? Don't you know that I am an outlaw and may not leave the forest?"

Abbot Hans looked him fearlessly in the eyes. "It is my purpose to get a letter of ransom for you from Archbishop Absalon," said he. He had hardly finished speaking when the robber and his wife burst out laughing. They knew well enough the kind of mercy a forest robber could expect from Bishop Absalon!

"Oh, if I get a letter of ransom from Absalon," said Robber Father, "then I'll promise you that never again will I steal so much as a goose."

Suddenly Robber Mother rose. "You sit here and talk, Abbot Hans," she said, "so that we are forgetting to look at the forest. Now I can hear, even in this cave, how the Christmas bells are ringing."

The words were barely uttered when they all sprang up and rushed out. But in the forest it was still dark night and bleak winter. The only thing they marked was a distant clang borne on a light south wind.

When the bells had been ringing a few moments, a sudden illumination penetrated the forest; the next moment it was dark again, and then light came back. It pushed its way forward between the stark trees, like a shimmering mist. The darkness merged into a faint daybreak. Then Abbot Hans saw that the snow had vanished from the ground, as if someone had removed a carpet, and the earth began to take on a green covering. The

moss-tufts thickened and raised themselves, and the spring blossoms shot upward their swelling buds, which already had a touch of color.

Again it grew hazy; but almost immediately there came a new wave of light. Then the leaves of the trees burst into bloom, crossbeaks hopped from branch to branch, and the woodpeckers hammered on the limbs until the splinters fairly flew around them. A flock of starlings from up country lighted in a fir top to rest.

When the next warm wind came along, the blueberries ripened and the baby squirrels began playing on the branches of the trees.

The next light wave that came rushing in brought with it the scent of newly ploughed acres. Pine and spruce trees were so thickly clothed with red cones that they shone like crimson mantles and forest flowers covered the ground till it was all red, blue, and yellow.

Abbot Hans bent down to the earth and broke off a wild strawberry blossom, and, as he straightened up, the berry ripened in his hand.

The mother fox came out of her lair with a big litter of black-legged young. She went up to Robber Mother and scratched at her skirt, and Robber Mother bent down to her and praised her young.

Robber Mother's youngsters let out perfect shrieks of delight. They stuffed themselves with wild strawberries that hung on the bushes. One of them played with a litter of young hares; another ran a race with some young crows, which had hopped from their nest before they were really ready.

Robber Father was standing out on a marsh eat-

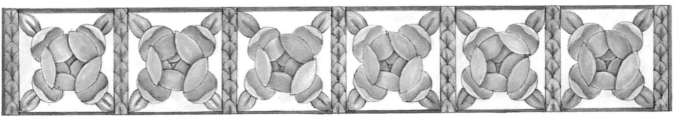

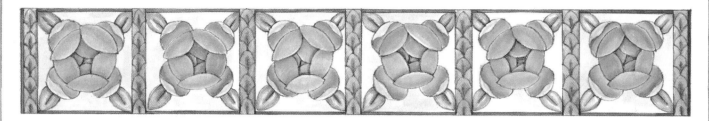

ing raspberries. When he glanced up, a big black bear stood beside him. Robber Father broke off a twig and struck the bear on the nose. "Keep to your own ground, you!" he said; "this is my turf." The huge bear turned around and lumbered off in another direction.

Then all the flowers whose seeds had been brought from foreign lands began to blossom. The loveliest roses climbed up the mountain wall in a race with the blackberry vines, and from the forest meadow sprang flowers as large as human faces.

Abbot Hans thought of the flower he was to pluck for Bishop Absalon; but each new flower that appeared was more beautiful than the others, and he wanted to choose the most beautiful of all.

Then Abbot Hans marked how all grew still; the birds hushed their songs, the flowers ceased growing, and the young foxes played no more. From far in the distance faint harp tones were heard, and celestial song, like a soft murmur, reached him.

He clasped his hands and dropped to his knees. His face was radiant with bliss.

But beside Abbot Hans stood the lay brother who had accompanied him. In his mind there were dark thoughts. "This cannot be a true miracle," he thought, "since it is revealed to malfactors. This does not come from God, but is sent hither by Satan. It is the Evil One's power that is tempting us and compelling us to see that which has no real existence."

The angel throng was so near now that Abbot Hans saw their bright forms through the forest branches. The lay brother saw them, too; but back of all this wondrous beauty he saw only some dread evil.

All the while the birds had been circling around the head of Abbot Hans, and they let him take them in his hands. But all the animals were afraid of the lay brother; no bird perched on his shoulder, no snake played at his feet. Then there came a little forest dove. When she marked that the angels were nearing, she plucked up courage and flew down on the lay brother's shoulder and laid her head against his cheek.

Then it appeared to him as if sorcery were come right upon him, to tempt and corrupt him. He struck with his hand at the forest dove and cried in such a loud voice that it rang throughout the forest, "Go thou back to hell, whence thou art come!"

Just then the angels were so near that Abbot Hans felt the feathery touch of their great wings, and he bowed down to earth in reverent greeting.

But when the lay brother's words sounded, their song was hushed and the holy guests turned in flight. At the same time the light and the mild warmth vanished in unspeakable terror for the darkness and cold in a human heart. Darkness sank over the earth, like a coverlet; frost came, all the growths shrivelled up; the animals and birds hastened away; the leaves dropped from the trees, rustling like rain.

Abbot Hans felt how his heart, which had but lately swelled with bliss, was now contracting with insufferable agony. "I can never outlive this," thought he, "that the angels from heaven had been so close to me and were driven away; that they wanted to sing Christmas carols for me and were driven to flight."

Then he remembered the flower he had promised Bishop Absalon, and at the last moment he fumbled among the leaves and moss to try and find a blossom. But he sensed how the ground under his fingers froze and how the white snow came gliding over the ground. Then his heart caused him even greater anguish. He could not rise, but fell prostrate on the ground and lay there.

When the robber folk and the lay brother had groped their way back to the cave, they missed

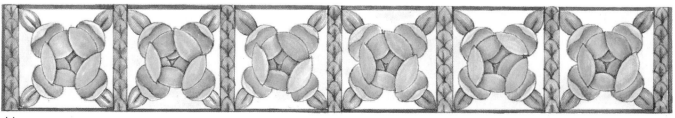

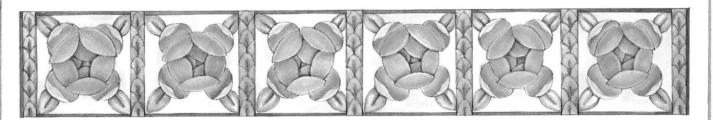

Abbot Hans. They took brands with them and went out to search for him. They found him dead upon the coverlet of snow.

When Abbot Hans had been carried down to Övid, those who took charge of the dead saw that he held his right hand locked tight around something which he must have grasped at the moment of death. When they finally got his hand open, they found that the thing which he had held in such an iron grip was a pair of white root bulbs, which he had torn from among the moss and leaves.

When the lay brother who had accompanied Abbot Hans saw the bulbs, he took them and planted them in Abbot Hans' herb garden.

He guarded them the whole year to see if any flower would spring from them. But in vain he waited through the spring, the summer, and the autumn. Finally, when winter had set in and all the leaves and flowers were dead, he ceased caring for them.

But when Christmas Eve came again, he was so strongly reminded of Abbot Hans that he wandered out into the garden to think of him. And look! as he came to the spot where he had planted the bare root bulbs, he saw that from them had sprung flourishing green stalks, which bore beautiful flowers with silver white leaves.

He called out all the monks at Övid, and when they saw that this plant bloomed on Christmas Eve, when all the other growths were as if dead, they understood that this flower had in truth been plucked by Abbot Hans from the Christmas garden in Göinge forest. Then the lay brother asked the monks if he might take a few blossoms to Bishop Absalon.

When Bishop Absalon beheld the flowers, which had sprung from the earth in darkest winter, he turned as pale as if he had met a ghost. He sat in silence a moment; thereupon he said, "Abbot Hans has faithfully kept his word and I shall also keep mine."

He handed the letter of ransom to the lay brother, who departed at once for the Robbers' Cave. When he stepped in there on Christmas Day, the robber came toward him with axe uplifted. "I'd like to hack you monks into bits, as many as you are!" said he. "It must be your fault that Göinge forest did not last night dress itself in Christmas bloom."

"The fault is mine alone," said the lay brother, "and I will gladly die for it; but first I must deliver a message from Abbot Hans." And he drew forth the Bishop's letter and told the man that he was free.

Robber Father stood there pale and speechless, but Robber Mother said in his name, "Abbot Hans has indeed kept his word, and Robber Father will keep his."

When the robber and his wife left the cave, the lay brother moved in and lived all alone in the forest, in constant meditation and prayer that his hard-heartedness might be forgiven him.

But Göinge forest never again celebrated the hour of our Savior's birth; and of all its glory, there lives today only the plant which Abbot Hans had plucked. It has been named CHRISTMAS ROSE. And each year at Christmastide she sends forth from the earth her green stalks and white blossoms, as if she never could forget that she had once grown in the great Christmas garden at Göinge forest.

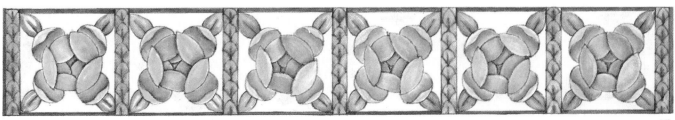

Our Joyful'st Feast

So now is come our joyful'st feast;
Let every man be jolly.
Each room with ivy-leaves is dressed,
And every post with holly.
    Though some churls at our mirth repine
    Round your foreheads garlands twine,
    Drown sorrow in a cup of wine,
And let us all be merry.

Now all our neighbours' chimneys smoke,
And Christmas blocks are burning;
The ovens they with baked meats choke,
And all their spits are turning.
    Without the door let sorrow lie,
    And if for cold it hap to die,
    We'll bury 't in a Christmas pie,
And evermore be merry.

Now every lad is wondrous trim,
And no man minds his labour;
Our lasses have provided them
A bag-pipe and a tabor.
    Young men, and maids, and girls and boys,
    Give life to one another's joys,
    And you anon shall by their noise
Perceive that they are merry.

Rank misers now do sparing shun,
Their hall of music soundeth,
And dogs thence with whole shoulders run,
So all things there aboundeth.
    The country-folk themselves advance,
    For crowdy-mutton's come out of France;
    And Jack shall pipe, and Jill shall dance,
And all the town be merry. . . .

The wenches with their wassail bowls
About the streets are singing,
The boys are come to catch the owls,
The wild mare in is bringing.
   Our kitchen-boy hath broke his box,
   And to the dealing of the ox
   Our honest neighbours come by flocks,
And here they will be merry. . . .

Then wherefore in these merry days
Should we, I pray, be duller?
No; let us sing our roundelays
To make our mirth the fuller.
   And, whilst thus inspired we sing,
   Let all the streets with echoes ring;
   Woods, and hills, and everything,
Bear witness we are merry.

Christmas Recipes

Cranberry Relish

MAKES 3 CUPS

This terrific side dish goes with any holiday meat or bird. It will keep refrigerated for several weeks, or can be preserved and given as a holiday gift.

INGREDIENTS

3 quarts water

6 whole cloves

1 teaspoon cinnamon

½ teaspoon mace

2 medium onions, chopped

6 cups fresh cranberries

2 cups pecan pieces

¾ cup apple cider vinegar

¾ cup brown sugar

½ cup clear corn syrup

METHOD

1. Boil water with spices and onions, then simmer 5 minutes.
2. Wash cranberries. Add to simmering water. When berries begin to soften and burst, remove from heat. When steam clears, place mixture in food processor. "Whiz" into a coarse puree. Return mixture to pot.
3. Coarsely chop pecan pieces and add to pot. Add vinegar, brown sugar, and corn syrup. Bring to boil, then reduce to simmer. Simmer 45 minutes, stirring occasionally.

Serve warmed, room temperature, or chilled.

Champagne-Oyster Bisque with Leeks

SERVES 6

INGREDIENTS

4 Tablespoons unsalted butter

3 medium leeks (greens only), washed, trimmed, and finely diced

1 cup champagne

3 cups oyster juice (comes with oysters; use clam broth if more juice is needed)

2 cups heavy cream

salt and freshly cracked black pepper

3 dozen shucked oysters

3 Tablespoons softened butter

⅛ cup chopped chives

METHOD

1. Melt butter in sauce pan over medium-low heat. Add diced leeks. Cook until leeks soften and become transparent.
2. Add champagne. Raise heat to medium-high. Cook until mixture becomes thick and reduces by ⅓.
3. Add oyster (and clam) juice. Let cook until mixture reduces by ⅓.
4. Add cream. Bring to boil, then reduce heat to high simmer. Let soup reduce ⅓. Season with salt and pepper.
5. Mix softened butter with chives. Set aside until ready to serve.
6. Warm 6 soup bowls. Divide oysters into bowls. Pour bisque into bowls. Add a dollop of chive butter.

Our Christmas Menu

Our Favorite Christmas Recipes

Our Yuletide Guests

Our Yuletide Memories

_____
_____
_____
_____
_____
_____
_____
_____
_____
_____
_____
_____
_____
_____
_____
_____
_____
_____

Pictures of Christmas

Christmas Gifts Received

Thank-you
Note Sent

Thoughts for the New Year